HO, HO, HO!

MERRY MAD LIBS®!

Mad Libs
An Imprint of Penguin Random House

MAD LIBS
Penguin Young Readers Group
An Imprint of Penguin Random House LLC

Mad Libs format and text copyright © 2003, 2007, 2010, 2017 by Penguin Random House LLC.
All rights reserved.

Concept created by Roger Price & Leonard Stern

Ho, Ho, Ho! Merry Mad Libs! published in 2017 by Mad Libs,
an imprint of Penguin Random House LLC,
345 Hudson Street, New York, New York 10014.
Manufactured in China.

Ho, Ho, Ho! Merry Mad Libs! ISBN 9781524786533
1 3 5 7 9 10 8 6 4 2

MAD LIBS®
INSTRUCTIONS

MAD LIBS® is a game for people who don't like games! It can be played by one, two, three, four, or forty.

● RIDICULOUSLY SIMPLE DIRECTIONS

In this tablet you will find stories containing blank spaces where words are left out. One player, the READER, selects one of these stories. The READER does not tell anyone what the story is about. Instead, he/she asks the other players, the WRITERS, to give him/her words. These words are used to fill in the blank spaces in the story.

● TO PLAY

The READER asks each WRITER in turn to call out a word—an adjective or a noun or whatever the space calls for—and uses them to fill in the blank spaces in the story. The result is a MAD LIBS® game.

When the READER then reads the completed MAD LIBS® game to the other players, they will discover that they have written a story that is fantastic, screamingly funny, shocking, silly, crazy, or just plain dumb—depending upon which words each WRITER called out.

● EXAMPLE (*Before* and *After*)

" _____ !" he said _____
      EXCLAMATION   ADVERB

as he jumped into his convertible _____ and
                                                NOUN

drove off with his _____ wife.
                          ADJECTIVE

" __OUCH__ !" he said __STUPIDLY__
      EXCLAMATION   ADVERB

as he jumped into his convertible __CAT__ and
                                              NOUN

drove off with his __BRAVE__ wife.
                          ADJECTIVE

In case you have forgotten what adjectives, adverbs, nouns, and verbs are, here is a quick review:

An ADJECTIVE describes something or somebody. *Lumpy, soft, ugly, messy,* and *short* are adjectives.

An ADVERB tells how something is done. It modifies a verb and usually ends in "ly." *Modestly, stupidly, greedily,* and *carefully* are adverbs.

A NOUN is the name of a person, place, or thing. *Sidewalk, umbrella, bridle, bathtub,* and *nose* are nouns.

A VERB is an action word. *Run, pitch, jump,* and *swim* are verbs. Put the verbs in past tense if the directions say PAST TENSE. *Ran, pitched, jumped,* and *swam* are verbs in the past tense.

When we ask for A PLACE, we mean any sort of place: a country or city (*Spain, Cleveland*) or a room (*bathroom, kitchen*).

An EXCLAMATION or SILLY WORD is any sort of funny sound, gasp, grunt, or outcry, like *Wow!, Ouch!, Whomp!, Ick!,* and *Gadzooks!*

When we ask for specific words, like a NUMBER, a COLOR, an ANIMAL, or a PART OF THE BODY, we mean a word that is one of those things, like *seven, blue, horse,* or *head.*

When we ask for a PLURAL, it means more than one. For example, *cat* pluralized is *cats.*

CHRISTMAS CAROL
MAD LIBS

VERY MERRY
SONGS & STORIES

Mad Libs
An Imprint of Penguin Random House

MAD LIBS® is fun to play with friends, but you can also play it by yourself! To begin with, DO NOT look at the story on the page below. Fill in the blanks on this page with the words called for. Then, using the words you have selected, fill in the blank spaces in the story.

Now you've created your own hilarious MAD LIBS® game!

JINGLE BELLS

PLURAL NOUN _____

ANIMAL _____

NOUN _____

PLURAL NOUN _____

VERB ENDING IN "ING" _____

PLURAL NOUN _____

PLURAL NOUN _____

VERB _____

PLURAL NOUN _____

SAME PLURAL NOUN _____

VERB _____

SAME ANIMAL _____

MAD LIBS

JINGLE BELLS

Dashing through the _____,
_____PLURAL NOUN_____

In a one-_____ open _____,
_____ANIMAL_____ _____NOUN_____

O'er the _____ we go,
_____PLURAL NOUN_____

_____ all the way.
VERB ENDING IN "ING"

_____ on bobtails ring,
PLURAL NOUN

Making _____ bright.
PLURAL NOUN

What fun it is to _____ and sing
_____VERB_____

A sleighing song tonight!

Jingle _____, jingle _____,
PLURAL NOUN _SAME PLURAL NOUN_

Jingle all the way!

Oh, what fun it is to _____
_____VERB_____

In a one-_____ open sleigh.
SAME ANIMAL

MAD LIBS® is fun to play with friends, but you can also play it by yourself! To begin with, DO NOT look at the story on the page below. Fill in the blanks on this page with the words called for. Then, using the words you have selected, fill in the blank spaces in the story.

Now you've created your own hilarious MAD LIBS® game!

GOING CAROLING

ADJECTIVE _____

ADJECTIVE _____

NUMBER _____

ADJECTIVE _____

PLURAL NOUN _____

PLURAL NOUN _____

ADJECTIVE _____

PLURAL NOUN _____

NOUN _____

PLURAL NOUN _____

VERB _____

NUMBER _____

NOUN _____

NUMBER _____

ADVERB _____

NOUN _____

PLURAL NOUN _____

VERB _____

MAD LIBS®

GOING CAROLING

'Tis the _____ season for caroling! Here's how to make
         ADJECTIVE

everyone's Christmas a little more merry and _____:
                                              ADJECTIVE

- Gather _____ of your _____ friends and
          NUMBER   ADJECTIVE

  family _____ together. Pick out a few classic
          PLURAL NOUN

  _____ to sing, like "Have Yourself a/an
   PLURAL NOUN

  _____ Little Christmas," "Silver _____,"
   ADJECTIVE   PLURAL NOUN

  and "Frosty the _____-man."
                    NOUN

- Put Santa _____ on everyone's heads and
             PLURAL NOUN

  _____ to your neighbor's house.
   VERB

- Knock _____ times on the front _____. Nothing?
         NUMBER   NOUN

  Knock _____ more times _____.
         NUMBER   ADVERB

- When your neighbor answers the _____, ask if he or she
                                  NOUN

  would like to hear you sing a song. If your neighbor says yes, sing

  your _____ out. If your neighbor says no, _____
        PLURAL NOUN   VERB

  anyway!

MAD LIBS® is fun to play with friends, but you can also play it by yourself! To begin with, DO NOT look at the story on the page below. Fill in the blanks on this page with the words called for. Then, using the words you have selected, fill in the blank spaces in the story.

Now you've created your own hilarious MAD LIBS® game!

DECK THE HALLS

PLURAL NOUN _____

PLURAL NOUN _____

NOUN _____

ADJECTIVE _____

ADJECTIVE _____

ADJECTIVE _____

VERB ENDING IN "ING" _____

NOUN _____

ADJECTIVE _____

ADJECTIVE _____

MAD LIBS

DECK THE HALLS

Deck the _____ with boughs of _____,
            PLURAL NOUN   PLURAL NOUN

Fa-la-la-la-la-la-la-la-la!

'Tis the _____ to be _____,
              NOUN   ADJECTIVE

Fa-la-la-la-la-la-la-la-la!

Don we now our _____ apparel,
                      ADJECTIVE

Fa-la-la-la-la-la-la-la-la!

Troll the ancient _____ carol,
                        ADJECTIVE

Fa-la-la-la-la-la-la-la-la!

See the _____ Yule before us,
          VERB ENDING IN "ING"

Fa-la-la-la-la-la-la-la-la!

Strike the _____ and join the chorus,
                  NOUN

Fa-la-la-la-la-la-la-la-la!

Follow me in _____ measure,
                    ADJECTIVE

Fa-la-la-la-la-la-la-la-la!

While I tell of _____ treasure,
                      ADJECTIVE

Fa-la-la-la-la-la-la-la-la!

MAD LIBS® is fun to play with friends, but you can also play it by yourself! To begin with, DO NOT look at the story on the page below. Fill in the blanks on this page with the words called for. Then, using the words you have selected, fill in the blank spaces in the story.

Now you've created your own hilarious MAD LIBS® game!

THE TWELVE DAYS OF CHRISTMAS, PART 1

NOUN _____

NOUN _____

NOUN _____

ADJECTIVE _____

NOUN _____

ADJECTIVE _____

ADJECTIVE _____

NOUN _____

PLURAL NOUN _____

ADJECTIVE _____

NOUN _____

On the first day of Christmas,

My true _____ gave to me
NOUN

A partridge in a/an _____ tree.
NOUN

On the second _____ of Christmas,
NOUN

My _____ love gave to me
ADJECTIVE

Two turtle doves

And a/an _____ in a/an _____ tree.
NOUN   ADJECTIVE

On the third day of Christmas,

My _____ _____ gave to me
ADJECTIVE   NOUN

Three French hens,

Two turtle _____,
PLURAL NOUN

And a partridge in a/an _____ _____.
ADJECTIVE   NOUN

MAD LIBS® is fun to play with friends, but you can also play it by yourself! To begin with, DO NOT look at the story on the page below. Fill in the blanks on this page with the words called for. Then, using the words you have selected, fill in the blank spaces in the story.

Now you've created your own hilarious MAD LIBS® game!

THE TWELVE DAYS OF CHRISTMAS, PART 2

NOUN _____

NUMBER _____

ADJECTIVE _____

NOUN _____

ADJECTIVE _____

NOUN _____

PLURAL NOUN _____

PLURAL NOUN _____

ADJECTIVE _____

PLURAL NOUN _____

ADJECTIVE _____

PLURAL NOUN _____

NOUN _____

ADJECTIVE _____

NOUN _____

MAD LIBS®
THE TWELVE DAYS
OF CHRISTMAS, PART 2

On the fourth day of Christmas,

My true _____ gave to me
NOUN

Four calling birds,

_____ French hens,
NUMBER

Two _____ doves,
ADJECTIVE

And a/an _____ in a pear tree.
NOUN

On the fifth day of Christmas,

My _____ _____ gave to me
ADJECTIVE   NOUN

Five golden _____,
PLURAL NOUN

Four calling _____,
PLURAL NOUN

Three _____ _____,
ADJECTIVE   PLURAL NOUN

Two _____ _____,
ADJECTIVE   PLURAL NOUN

And a/an _____ in a/an _____ _____.
NOUN   ADJECTIVE   NOUN

MAD LIBS® is fun to play with friends, but you can also play it by yourself! To begin with, DO NOT look at the story on the page below. Fill in the blanks on this page with the words called for. Then, using the words you have selected, fill in the blank spaces in the story.

Now you've created your own hilarious MAD LIBS® game!

CHRISTMAS SHOPPING

ADJECTIVE _____

ADJECTIVE _____

PLURAL NOUN _____

NOUN _____

CELEBRITY _____

VERB (PAST TENSE) _____

VERB _____

ADJECTIVE _____

NOUN _____

TYPE OF LIQUID _____

ADJECTIVE _____

ADJECTIVE _____

NOUN _____

PLURAL NOUN _____

PLURAL NOUN _____

PLURAL NOUN _____

PLURAL NOUN _____

NOUN _____

VERB ENDING IN "ING" _____

MAD LIBS

CHRISTMAS SHOPPING

When I was a/an _____ kid, I loved going to the _____
                    ADJECTIVE   ADJECTIVE

mall at Christmastime. My parents would dress me and my

_____ in our cutest holiday outfits. Then we'd all pile into
PLURAL NOUN

the family _____ and drive to the mall to sit on
                    NOUN

_____'s lap. As we _____ in the long line to
CELEBRITY   VERB (PAST TENSE)

Santa's _____-shop, we'd look around at all the
                    VERB

_____ lights strung around the _____, drink hot
ADJECTIVE   NOUN

_____, and sing _____ carols. Then the
TYPE OF LIQUID   ADJECTIVE

_____ moment would arrive—we'd finally get to meet Santa
ADJECTIVE

and tell him what we wanted to find under the _____ on
                                                    NOUN

Christmas morning. Of course, now that I'm older, I avoid the mall at

all _____. It's so crowded that all the _____
    PLURAL NOUN   PLURAL NOUN

push into one another. You can't even catch of glimpse of Santa and his

_____. These days, I buy all my _____ online.
PLURAL NOUN   PLURAL NOUN

With just a click of the _____, Christmas
                              NOUN

_____ couldn't be easier!
VERB ENDING IN "ING"

MAD LIBS® is fun to play with friends, but you can also play it by yourself! To begin with, DO NOT look at the story on the page below. Fill in the blanks on this page with the words called for. Then, using the words you have selected, fill in the blank spaces in the story.

Now you've created your own hilarious MAD LIBS® game!

THE CHRISTMAS PAGEANT

ADJECTIVE _____

A PLACE _____

PLURAL NOUN _____

PLURAL NOUN _____

ADJECTIVE _____

NOUN _____

NOUN _____

SILLY WORD _____

PERSON IN ROOM (MALE) _____

NOUN _____

ADJECTIVE _____

ADJECTIVE _____

COLOR _____

NOUN _____

ADJECTIVE _____

PART OF THE BODY (PLURAL) _____

PLURAL NOUN _____

SILLY WORD _____

MAD LIBS®

THE CHRISTMAS PAGEANT

Every December, our school puts on a/an _____ holiday
_{ADJECTIVE}

pageant. We decorate (the) _____ with snow-_____
_{A PLACE} _{PLURAL NOUN}

and red and green _____, and we perform a/an
_{PLURAL NOUN}

_____ play and sing Christmas carols. This year, the
_{ADJECTIVE}

_____ is set in the North Pole. Our music _____,
_{NOUN} _{NOUN}

Mrs. _____, cast my best friend, _____, as
_{SILLY WORD} _{PERSON IN ROOM (MALE)}

Santa. He will, of course, be wearing a red _____ stuffed with
_{NOUN}

a/an _____ pillow so he'll look really _____. I was
_{ADJECTIVE} _{ADJECTIVE}

cast as Rudolph the _____ -nosed _____. I'll be
_{COLOR} _{NOUN}

wearing _____ antlers on my _____. The
_{ADJECTIVE} _{PART OF THE BODY (PLURAL)}

rest of the class will be elves making _____ in Santa's
_{PLURAL NOUN}

workshop. I can't wait! Ho, _____, ho!
_{SILLY WORD}

MAD LIBS® is fun to play with friends, but you can also play it by yourself! To begin with, DO NOT look at the story on the page below. Fill in the blanks on this page with the words called for. Then, using the words you have selected, fill in the blank spaces in the story.

Now you've created your own hilarious MAD LIBS® game!

O CHRISTMAS TREE

NOUN _____

SAME NOUN _____

ADJECTIVE _____

SAME NOUN _____

SAME NOUN _____

ADJECTIVE _____

ADJECTIVE _____

PLURAL NOUN _____

ADJECTIVE _____

PLURAL NOUN _____

SAME NOUN _____

SAME NOUN _____

ADJECTIVE _____

MAD LIBS®

O CHRISTMAS TREE

O Christmas _____, O Christmas _____,
          NOUN   SAME NOUN

How _____ are your branches!
        ADJECTIVE

O Christmas _____, O Christmas _____,
          SAME NOUN   SAME NOUN

How _____ are your branches!
        ADJECTIVE

They're _____ when summer _____ are bright,
          ADJECTIVE   PLURAL NOUN

They're _____ when winter _____ are white.
          ADJECTIVE   PLURAL NOUN

O Christmas _____, O Christmas _____,
          SAME NOUN   SAME NOUN

How _____ are your branches!
        ADJECTIVE

MAD LIBS® is fun to play with friends, but you can also play it by yourself! To begin with, DO NOT look at the story on the page below. Fill in the blanks on this page with the words called for. Then, using the words you have selected, fill in the blank spaces in the story.

Now you've created your own hilarious MAD LIBS® game!

UP ON THE HOUSETOP

NOUN _____

ANIMAL (PLURAL) _____

ADJECTIVE _____

NOUN _____

ADJECTIVE _____

PERSON IN ROOM _____

PLURAL NOUN _____

EXCLAMATION _____

NOUN _____

VERB _____

PERSON IN ROOM _____

NOUN _____

SILLY WORD _____

SAME SILLY WORD _____

SAME SILLY WORD _____

ADJECTIVE _____

MAD LIBS

UP ON THE HOUSETOP

Up on the _____-top, _____ pause,
         NOUN   ANIMAL (PLURAL)

Out jumps _____ old Santa Claus.
         ADJECTIVE

Down through the _____ with lots of toys,
           NOUN

All for the _____ ones, Christmas joys.
        ADJECTIVE

Ho, ho, ho! Who wouldn't go? Ho, ho, ho! _____ wouldn't go!
                                         PERSON IN ROOM

First comes the _____ of little Nell.
          PLURAL NOUN

_____ ! Dear Santa, fill it well!
 EXCLAMATION

Give her a/an _____ that laughs and cries,
           NOUN

One that will _____ and shut its eyes.
         VERB

Ho, ho, ho! Who wouldn't go? Ho, ho, ho! _____ wouldn't go!
                                         PERSON IN ROOM

Up on the _____-top, _____, _____,
         NOUN   SILLY WORD   SAME SILLY WORD

_____ !
 SAME SILLY WORD

Down through the chimney with _____ Saint Nick.
                               ADJECTIVE

MAD LIBS® is fun to play with friends, but you can also play it by yourself! To begin with, DO NOT look at the story on the page below. Fill in the blanks on this page with the words called for. Then, using the words you have selected, fill in the blank spaces in the story.

Now you've created your own hilarious MAD LIBS® game!

A CHRISTMAS SOLO

NOUN _____

ADVERB _____

ADJECTIVE _____

VERB ENDING IN "ING" _____

NUMBER _____

NOUN _____

VERB (PAST TENSE) _____

COLOR _____

PART OF THE BODY _____

PERSON IN ROOM _____

ADJECTIVE _____

PLURAL NOUN _____

ADJECTIVE _____

PLURAL NOUN _____

ADJECTIVE _____

VERB (PAST TENSE) _____

SAME VERB (PAST TENSE) _____

NOUN _____

ADJECTIVE _____

MAD LIBS®

A CHRISTMAS SOLO

A few years ago, my music _____ asked me to sing a Christmas
                              NOUN

solo at our holiday concert. At first I was _____ flattered, but
                                              ADVERB

the more I thought about it, the more _____ I became. Every
                                          ADJECTIVE

time I thought about _____ in front of _____
                      VERB ENDING IN "ING"   NUMBER

people, my whole _____ started to shake. What if I
                    NOUN

_____ or forgot the lyrics? What if I suddenly
VERB (PAST TENSE)

developed a/an _____ rash on my _____? My friend
                  COLOR   PART OF THE BODY

_____ suggested picturing the audience as a bunch of
PERSON IN ROOM

_____ _____ to make it easier. That seemed like
ADJECTIVE   PLURAL NOUN

a/an _____ plan—until I worried I'd start laughing and all the
        ADJECTIVE

_____ would think I was _____. Finally, the
PLURAL NOUN   ADJECTIVE

night of the concert arrived. I walked onstage, gathered all my courage,

and _____ like I'd never _____
      VERB (PAST TENSE)   SAME VERB (PAST TENSE)

before. The song went off without a/an _____, and I received
                                          NOUN

a standing ovation. It was the most _____ moment of my
                                        ADJECTIVE

entire life!

MAD LIBS® is fun to play with friends, but you can also play it by yourself! To begin with, DO NOT look at the story on the page below. Fill in the blanks on this page with the words called for. Then, using the words you have selected, fill in the blank spaces in the story.

Now you've created your own hilarious MAD LIBS® game!

AUNTIE'S CRAZY CHRISTMAS CLOTHING

PLURAL NOUN _____

PLURAL NOUN _____

ADJECTIVE _____

PERSON IN ROOM (FEMALE) _____

ADJECTIVE _____

PLURAL NOUN _____

PLURAL NOUN _____

PART OF THE BODY _____

PLURAL NOUN _____

COLOR _____

A PLACE _____

NOUN _____

PART OF THE BODY _____

VERB (PAST TENSE) _____

PART OF THE BODY _____

MAD LIBS®
AUNTIE'S CRAZY
CHRISTMAS CLOTHING

Every Christmas, my family gets together to exchange _____

PLURAL NOUN

and eat a big Christmas dinner of ham, mashed _____,

PLURAL NOUN

and all the _____ trimmings. For me, though, the highlight of

ADJECTIVE

every Christmas is seeing my aunt _____ make her

PERSON IN ROOM (FEMALE)

_____ entrance. She always wears the craziest _____

ADJECTIVE   PLURAL NOUN

on Christmas. You wouldn't believe it! For example, last year she wore

earrings that looked like giant Christmas _____, a

PLURAL NOUN

sweatshirt with Santa's _____ on the front, and socks with

PART OF THE BODY

red-and-white candy _____ on them. She also wore a

PLURAL NOUN

snowflake pin with a flashing _____ light that played "Santa

COLOR

Claus Is Coming to (the) _____," and she carried a/an

A PLACE

_____ made out of tinsel. To top it all off, she tied bells to her

NOUN

_____ so she would jingle when she _____!

PART OF THE BODY   VERB (PAST TENSE)

Gosh, that was almost as funny as the year she wrapped her entire

_____ in Christmas lights! I can't wait to see what she'll wear

PART OF THE BODY

this year.

MAD LIBS® is fun to play with friends, but you can also play it by yourself! To begin with, DO NOT look at the story on the page below. Fill in the blanks on this page with the words called for. Then, using the words you have selected, fill in the blank spaces in the story.

Now you've created your own hilarious MAD LIBS® game!

'TWAS THE NIGHT BEFORE CHRISTMAS, PART 1

NOUN _____

ANIMAL _____

PLURAL NOUN _____

CELEBRITY (MALE) _____

ADJECTIVE _____

NUMBER _____

ADJECTIVE _____

ADJECTIVE _____

SAME CELEBRITY (MALE) _____

PLURAL NOUN _____

VERB (PAST TENSE) _____

VERB (PAST TENSE) _____

PERSON IN ROOM _____

SILLY WORD _____

SILLY WORD _____

SILLY WORD _____

NOUN _____

VERB _____

VERB _____

VERB _____

MAD LIBS®
'TWAS THE NIGHT BEFORE CHRISTMAS, PART 1

'Twas the night before Christmas, when all through the _____,

NOUN

Not a creature was stirring, not even a/an _____.

ANIMAL

The _____ were hung by the chimney with care,

PLURAL NOUN

In hopes that _____ soon would be there.

CELEBRITY (MALE)

When, what to my wondering eyes should appear,

But a/an _____ sleigh and _____ _____ reindeer.

ADJECTIVE   NUMBER   ADJECTIVE

With a little old driver, so _____ and quick,

ADJECTIVE

I knew in a moment it must be _____.

SAME CELEBRITY (MALE)

More rapid than _____, his reindeer they came,

PLURAL NOUN

As he _____ and _____ and called

VERB (PAST TENSE)   VERB (PAST TENSE)

them by name:

"Now, _____! Now, Dancer! Now, _____ and Vixen!

PERSON IN ROOM   SILLY WORD

On, _____! On, Cupid! On, _____ and Blitzen!

SILLY WORD   SILLY WORD

To the top of the _____! To the top of the wall!

NOUN

Now _____ away! _____ away! _____ away, all!"

VERB   VERB   VERB

MAD LIBS® is fun to play with friends, but you can also play it by yourself! To begin with, DO NOT look at the story on the page below. Fill in the blanks on this page with the words called for. Then, using the words you have selected, fill in the blank spaces in the story.

Now you've created your own hilarious MAD LIBS® game!

'TWAS THE NIGHT BEFORE CHRISTMAS, PART 2

NOUN _____

VERB ENDING IN "ING" _____

VERB ENDING IN "ING" _____

ADJECTIVE _____

CELEBRITY _____

PLURAL NOUN _____

PLURAL NOUN _____

VERB (PAST TENSE) _____

PLURAL NOUN _____

VERB (PAST TENSE) _____

PART OF THE BODY _____

NOUN _____

VERB (PAST TENSE) _____

ADJECTIVE _____

ADJECTIVE _____

MAD⊙LIBS®
'TWAS THE NIGHT BEFORE CHRISTMAS, PART 2

And then in a twinkling, I heard on the _____,
                                         NOUN

The _____ and _____ of each
     VERB ENDING IN "ING"   VERB ENDING IN "ING"

_____ hoof.
  ADJECTIVE

And down the chimney _____ came, amid _____
                        CELEBRITY   PLURAL NOUN

and soot.

He was covered in _____ from his head to his foot.
                     PLURAL NOUN

He _____ not a word, but went straight to his work,
    VERB (PAST TENSE)

And filled all the _____, then _____ with
                     PLURAL NOUN   VERB (PAST TENSE)

a jerk.

And laying his _____ aside of his nose,
                 PART OF THE BODY

And giving a nod, up the _____ he rose!
                            NOUN

But I heard him exclaim as he _____ out of sight,
                                 VERB (PAST TENSE)

"_____ Christmas to all, and to all a/an _____
   ADJECTIVE   ADJECTIVE

night!"

MAD LIBS® is fun to play with friends, but you can also play it by yourself! To begin with, DO NOT look at the story on the page below. Fill in the blanks on this page with the words called for. Then, using the words you have selected, fill in the blank spaces in the story.

Now you've created your own hilarious MAD LIBS® game!

TOYLAND

NOUN _____

NOUN _____

NOUN _____

VERB _____

ADJECTIVE _____

NOUN _____

ADJECTIVE _____

ADJECTIVE _____

PLURAL NOUN _____

Toyland, _____-land,
_____ NOUN

Little _____ and _____ land,
_____ NOUN _____ NOUN

While you _____ within it,
_____ VERB

You are ever _____ there.
_____ ADJECTIVE

_____ joy land,
_____ NOUN

_____, _____ Toyland!
_____ ADJECTIVE _____ ADJECTIVE

Once you pass its _____,
_____ PLURAL NOUN

You can never return again.

MAD LIBS® is fun to play with friends, but you can also play it by yourself! To begin with, DO NOT look at the story on the page below. Fill in the blanks on this page with the words called for. Then, using the words you have selected, fill in the blank spaces in the story.

Now you've created your own hilarious MAD LIBS® game!

JOLLY OLD SAINT NICHOLAS

ADJECTIVE _____

PART OF THE BODY _____

NOUN _____

ADJECTIVE _____

NUMBER _____

NOUN _____

ADVERB _____

PLURAL NOUN _____

VERB ENDING IN "ING" _____

ADJECTIVE _____

PLURAL NOUN _____

NOUN _____

ADJECTIVE _____

VERB (PAST TENSE) _____

ADJECTIVE _____

MAD LIBS

JOLLY OLD SAINT NICHOLAS

Jolly _____ Saint Nicholas, lean your _____ this way!
    ADJECTIVE   PART OF THE BODY

Don't you tell a single _____ what I'm going to say.
                          NOUN

Christmas Eve is coming soon; now you dear _____ man,
                                              ADJECTIVE

Whisper what you'll bring to me; tell me if you can.

When the clock is striking _____, when I'm fast asleep,
                              NUMBER

Down the chimney with your _____, _____ you
                              NOUN   ADVERB

will creep.

All the _____ you will find, _____ in a row;
         PLURAL NOUN   VERB ENDING IN "ING"

Mine will be the _____ one—you'll be sure to know.
                   ADJECTIVE

Johnny wants a pair of _____, Susie wants a/an
                          PLURAL NOUN

_____,
    NOUN

Nellie wants a/an _____ book—one she hasn't _____.
                    ADJECTIVE   VERB (PAST TENSE)

Now I think I'll leave to you what to give the rest.

Choose for me, _____ Santa Claus. You will know the best.
                  ADJECTIVE

MAD LIBS® is fun to play with friends, but you can also play it by yourself! To begin with, DO NOT look at the story on the page below. Fill in the blanks on this page with the words called for. Then, using the words you have selected, fill in the blank spaces in the story.

Now you've created your own hilarious MAD LIBS® game!

OVER THE RIVER AND THROUGH THE WOOD

CELEBRITY _____

NOUN _____

NOUN _____

ADJECTIVE _____

ADJECTIVE _____

NOUN _____

NOUN _____

VERB _____

PART OF THE BODY (PLURAL) _____

PART OF THE BODY _____

NOUN _____

NOUN _____

NOUN _____

PLURAL NOUN _____

SILLY WORD _____

MAD LIBS
OVER THE RIVER AND THROUGH THE WOOD

Over the river and through the wood,

To _____'s house we go.
　　　　CELEBRITY

The _____ knows the way to carry the _____
　　　　NOUN　　　　　　　　　　　　　　　　　　　NOUN

Through the _____ and _____ snow.
　　　　　　　ADJECTIVE　　　　　ADJECTIVE

Over the _____ and through the _____,
　　　　　　NOUN　　　　　　　　　　　　　　NOUN

Oh, how the wind does _____.
　　　　　　　　　　　　　VERB

It stings the _____ and bites the _____
　　　　　　　PART OF THE BODY (PLURAL)　　　　　PART OF THE BODY

As over the _____ we go.
　　　　　　　NOUN

Over the river and through the _____,
　　　　　　　　　　　　　　　　NOUN

To have a full _____ of play.
　　　　　　　　NOUN

Oh, hear the _____ ringing _____-a-ling-ling,
　　　　　　　PLURAL NOUN　　　　　SILLY WORD

For it is Christmas Day!

MAD LIBS® is fun to play with friends, but you can also play it by yourself! To begin with, DO NOT look at the story on the page below. Fill in the blanks on this page with the words called for. Then, using the words you have selected, fill in the blank spaces in the story.

Now you've created your own hilarious MAD LIBS® game!

THE NAUGHTY LIST

ADJECTIVE _____

NOUN _____

ADJECTIVE _____

ADVERB _____

PLURAL NOUN _____

NOUN _____

PLURAL NOUN _____

ADJECTIVE _____

PLURAL NOUN _____

NOUN _____

PART OF THE BODY (PLURAL) _____

NOUN _____

NOUN _____

ADJECTIVE _____

SAME ADJECTIVE _____

MAD☺LIBS®

THE NAUGHTY LIST

Make sure you are always a/an _____ little girl or boy, or you
                                    ADJECTIVE

might get a lump of coal in your _____ at Christmas! Here is
                                        NOUN

a list of _____ things to do and *not* to do to stay off Santa's
              ADJECTIVE

naughty list:

ALWAYS play _____ with your brothers and/or sisters and
                      ADVERB

share your _____ with them.
                PLURAL NOUN

NEVER make a mess and then blame it on your pet _____.
                                                          NOUN

ALWAYS eat your green _____—even if they taste like
                              PLURAL NOUN

_____ _____.
   ADJECTIVE   PLURAL NOUN

ALWAYS make your _____ and brush your
                            NOUN

_____ every morning.
PART OF THE BODY (PLURAL)

NEVER tell your teacher that your _____ ate your
                                          NOUN

homework—unless, of course, you can bring in a well-chewed

_____ as proof.
   NOUN

And always remember: Santa knows when you've been bad or

_____, so be _____, for goodness' sake!
   ADJECTIVE   SAME ADJECTIVE

From CHRISTMAS CAROL MAD LIBS® • Copyright © 2003, 2007 by Penguin Random House LLC.

MAD LIBS® is fun to play with friends, but you can also play it by yourself! To begin with, DO NOT look at the story on the page below. Fill in the blanks on this page with the words called for. Then, using the words you have selected, fill in the blank spaces in the story.

Now you've created your own hilarious MAD LIBS® game!

FAVORITE CHRISTMAS CAROLS

ADVERB _____

VERB ENDING IN "ING" _____

ADJECTIVE _____

ADJECTIVE _____

NOUN _____

CELEBRITY _____

COLOR _____

VERB _____

NOUN _____

NOUN _____

NOUN _____

COLOR _____

NOUN _____

MAD⊙LIBS®
FAVORITE CHRISTMAS
CAROLS

Here's a list of the top ten most _____ played Christmas

ADVERB

carols. Which one is your favorite?

1. "The Christmas Song" ("Chestnuts _____

VERB ENDING IN "ING"

on a/an _____ Fire")

ADJECTIVE

2. "Have Yourself a Merry _____ Christmas"

ADJECTIVE

3. " _____ Wonderland"

NOUN

4. " _____ Is Coming to Town"

CELEBRITY

5. " _____ Christmas"

COLOR

6. "Let It _____"

VERB

7. "Jingle _____ Rock"

NOUN

8. "Little Drummer _____"

NOUN

9. " _____ Ride"

NOUN

10. "Rudolph the _____-Nosed _____"

COLOR   NOUN

MAD LIBS® is fun to play with friends, but you can also play it by yourself! To begin with, DO NOT look at the story on the page below. Fill in the blanks on this page with the words called for. Then, using the words you have selected, fill in the blank spaces in the story.

Now you've created your own hilarious MAD LIBS® game!

WE WISH YOU A MERRY CHRISTMAS

ADJECTIVE _____

SAME ADJECTIVE _____

SAME ADJECTIVE _____

ADJECTIVE _____

ADJECTIVE _____

PLURAL NOUN _____

ADJECTIVE _____

ADJECTIVE _____

ADJECTIVE _____

SAME ADJECTIVE _____

SAME ADJECTIVE _____

NOUN _____

VERB _____

SAME VERB _____

SAME VERB _____

VERB _____

MAD LIBS
WE WISH YOU A
MERRY CHRISTMAS

We wish you a/an _____ Christmas,
ADJECTIVE

We wish you a/an _____ Christmas,
SAME ADJECTIVE

We wish you a/an _____ Christmas
SAME ADJECTIVE

And a/an _____ New Year.
ADJECTIVE

_____ tidings we bring
ADJECTIVE

To you and your _____,
PLURAL NOUN

_____ tidings for Christmas
ADJECTIVE

And a/an _____ New Year.
ADJECTIVE

Oh, bring us a/an _____ pudding,
ADJECTIVE

Oh, bring us a/an _____ pudding,
SAME ADJECTIVE

Oh, bring us a/an _____ pudding
SAME ADJECTIVE

And a cup of good _____.
NOUN

We won't _____ until we get some,
VERB

We won't _____ until we get some,
SAME VERB

We won't _____ until we get some,
SAME VERB

So _____ some out here.
VERB

MAD LIBS® is fun to play with friends, but you can also play it by yourself! To begin with, DO NOT look at the story on the page below. Fill in the blanks on this page with the words called for. Then, using the words you have selected, fill in the blank spaces in the story.

Now you've created your own hilarious MAD LIBS® game!

A CHRISTMAS BLIZZARD

ADJECTIVE _____

ADJECTIVE _____

PLURAL NOUN _____

ADJECTIVE _____

VERB ENDING IN "ING" _____

ADJECTIVE _____

NOUN _____

NOUN _____

NOUN _____

NOUN _____

NOUN _____

NOUN _____

ADJECTIVE _____

MAD LIBS

A CHRISTMAS BLIZZARD

Have you been dreaming of a/an _____ Christmas? Me too!
                                    ADJECTIVE

But what do you do when there is a/an _____ blizzard and
                                              ADJECTIVE

you and your _____ get snowed in on Christmas? Here's
                  PLURAL NOUN

a/an _____ list of classic Christmas movies that'll keep
          ADJECTIVE

everyone _____ for hours.
              VERB ENDING IN "ING"

1. *It's a/an* _____ *Life*
                  ADJECTIVE

2. *Miracle on 34th* _____
                          NOUN

3. *A Christmas* _____
                      NOUN

4. *How the* _____ *Stole Christmas*
                  NOUN

5. *Frosty the Snow-*_____
                          NOUN

So just grab some pop-_____, throw a few more logs on the
                            NOUN

_____, and keep dreaming of a/an _____ white
      NOUN   ADJECTIVE

Christmas!

MAD LIBS® is fun to play with friends, but you can also play it by yourself! To begin with, DO NOT look at the story on the page below. Fill in the blanks on this page with the words called for. Then, using the words you have selected, fill in the blank spaces in the story.

Now you've created your own hilarious MAD LIBS® game!

HERE WE COME A-CAROLING

PLURAL NOUN _____

ADJECTIVE _____

VERB ENDING IN "ING" _____

ADJECTIVE _____

PLURAL NOUN _____

ADJECTIVE _____

ADJECTIVE _____

ADJECTIVE _____

NOUN _____

MAD LIBS®

HERE WE COME A-CAROLING

Here we come a-caroling among the _____ so _____.
                                        PLURAL NOUN   ADJECTIVE

Here we come a- _____ so _____ to be seen.
                  VERB ENDING IN "ING"   ADJECTIVE

Love and _____ come to you.
              PLURAL NOUN

And to you _____ Christmas, too.
                ADJECTIVE

And we wish you and send you a/an _____ New Year.
                                          ADJECTIVE

And we wish you a/an _____ New _____.
                          ADJECTIVE   NOUN

WE WISH YOU A MERRY MAD LIBS

Mad Libs
An Imprint of Penguin Random House

MAD LIBS® is fun to play with friends, but you can also play it by yourself! To begin with, DO NOT look at the story on the page below. Fill in the blanks on this page with the words called for. Then, using the words you have selected, fill in the blank spaces in the story.

Now you've created your own hilarious MAD LIBS® game!

VISIT THE NORTH POLE!

ADJECTIVE _____

ADJECTIVE _____

NOUN _____

ADVERB _____

ADJECTIVE _____

PART OF THE BODY (PLURAL) _____

NOUN _____

PLURAL NOUN _____

NOUN _____

ADJECTIVE _____

ADJECTIVE _____

ADJECTIVE _____

PLURAL NOUN _____

ADJECTIVE _____

PART OF THE BODY _____

PLURAL NOUN _____

MAD☺LIBS®

VISIT THE NORTH POLE!

Looking for a/an _____ destination for your next vacation?
<u>ADJECTIVE</u>

How about the _____ North Pole? Located in the middle of
<u>ADJECTIVE</u>

the Arctic _____, it is made up of _____ shifting ice,
<u>NOUN</u>   <u>ADVERB</u>

which makes it perfect for snowshoeing through the _____
<u>ADJECTIVE</u>

tundra. As you trek across the ice, keep your _____
<u>PART OF THE BODY (PLURAL)</u>

peeled for the incredible wildlife that inhabits the North

_____—like furry white polar _____,
<u>NOUN</u>   <u>PLURAL NOUN</u>

_____ seals, and _____ arctic foxes. And when night
<u>NOUN</u>   <u>ADJECTIVE</u>

falls, you are in for a/an _____ treat. You'll be able to see the
<u>ADJECTIVE</u>

_____ aurora borealis, otherwise known as the northern
<u>ADJECTIVE</u>

_____. This incredible display of _____ lights
<u>PLURAL NOUN</u>   <u>ADJECTIVE</u>

will blow your _____. So call 1-800-555-3939 and make
<u>PART OF THE BODY</u>

your travel _____ today!
<u>PLURAL NOUN</u>

MAD LIBS® is fun to play with friends, but you can also play it by yourself! To begin with, DO NOT look at the story on the page below. Fill in the blanks on this page with the words called for. Then, using the words you have selected, fill in the blank spaces in the story.

Now you've created your own hilarious MAD LIBS® game!

SANTA BLOG

ADJECTIVE _____

ADJECTIVE _____

NOUN _____

ADJECTIVE _____

A PLACE _____

NOUN _____

PLURAL NOUN _____

PLURAL NOUN _____

ADVERB _____

NOUN _____

ADJECTIVE _____

VERB _____

VERB _____

ADJECTIVE _____

ADJECTIVE _____

PLURAL NOUN _____

NOUN _____

MAD LIBS

SANTA BLOG

Ho, ho, ho, _____ blog fans! Santa here. It's crunch time at
             ADJECTIVE

my _____ workshop, and everyone is as busy as a/an
     ADJECTIVE

_____. I've received tons of _____ letters from girls
  NOUN   ADJECTIVE

and boys around (the) _____, and the elves have been working
            A PLACE

around the _____ to make all of their _____.
       NOUN   PLURAL NOUN

Plus, I've finally finished putting together the list of naughty

_____, which I'm _____ happy to say is much
  PLURAL NOUN   ADVERB

shorter than last year's! As I look out the _____, I can see the
                     NOUN

reindeer are groomed and look really _____, and my sleigh is
                ADJECTIVE

polished and ready to _____. I will be able to _____
         VERB   VERB

through the _____ night sky as soon as Mrs. Claus finishes
      ADJECTIVE

letting out my _____ red suit. I'm sorry to say, I ate a few too
       ADJECTIVE

many _____ this past year!
    PLURAL NOUN

See you soon! Your _____, Santa
           NOUN

MAD LIBS® is fun to play with friends, but you can also play it by yourself! To begin with, DO NOT look at the story on the page below. Fill in the blanks on this page with the words called for. Then, using the words you have selected, fill in the blank spaces in the story.

Now you've created your own hilarious MAD LIBS® game!

HOLIDAY WEATHER REPORT

ADJECTIVE _____

PERSON IN ROOM _____

NOUN _____

ADJECTIVE _____

ADJECTIVE _____

NUMBER _____

NOUN _____

NOUN _____

PLURAL NOUN _____

PLURAL NOUN _____

VERB ENDING IN "ING" _____

NUMBER _____

ADJECTIVE _____

PLURAL NOUN _____

VERB _____

NOUN _____

NOUN _____

ADJECTIVE _____

MAD☺LIBS®

HOLIDAY WEATHER REPORT

Good evening, and _____ holidays. I'm _____ with
                        ADJECTIVE   PERSON IN ROOM

your local weather _____. First the good news: We're going to
                        NOUN

have a traditional _____ Christmas. A/An _____
                        ADJECTIVE   ADJECTIVE

snowstorm is heading our way. You can expect three to _____
                                                            NUMBER

feet of _____ to accumulate before the end of this
            NOUN

_____, plus several more _____ of snow by
    NOUN   PLURAL NOUN

midnight. And you may want to put on your warm _____:
                                                    PLURAL NOUN

Overnight, the temperature is going to drop below _____
                                                    VERB ENDING IN "ING"

level, with a windchill of negative _____ degrees. Now the
                                        NUMBER

bad news: Driving conditions will be extremely _____. I
                                                    ADJECTIVE

strongly suggest you stay off the _____ and _____
                                    PLURAL NOUN   VERB

at home. Hunker down, light a/an _____ in the fireplace, and
                                    NOUN

watch the _____-flakes fall. And, most importantly, have a/an
            NOUN

_____ Christmas!
    ADJECTIVE

MAD LIBS® is fun to play with friends, but you can also play it by yourself! To begin with, DO NOT look at the story on the page below. Fill in the blanks on this page with the words called for. Then, using the words you have selected, fill in the blank spaces in the story.

Now you've created your own hilarious MAD LIBS® game!

MOST POPULAR GIFTS

ADJECTIVE _____

PLURAL NOUN _____

NOUN _____

ADJECTIVE _____

PLURAL NOUN _____

NOUN _____

NOUN _____

NOUN _____

NOUN _____

NOUN _____

ADJECTIVE _____

NOUN _____

PLURAL NOUN _____

ADJECTIVE _____

NOUN _____

ADJECTIVE _____

NOUN _____

NOUN _____

ADJECTIVE _____

NOUN _____

MAD LIBS®

MOST POPULAR GIFTS

Here is a list of the most _____ gifts for your dear _____:
ADJECTIVE   PLURAL NOUN

5. An i-_____. This _____ device can store
NOUN   ADJECTIVE

and play up to thirty thousand _____.
PLURAL NOUN

4. A/An _____-cam. Shoot movies or film yourself
NOUN

acting like a/an _____. Then, upload your videos to
NOUN

You-_____, where everyone can see them!
NOUN

3. *Rock* _____. Ever wanted to be a famous
NOUN

_____? You can act like one with this _____
NOUN   ADJECTIVE

video game.

2. A flat-screen _____. Watch your favorite movies and
NOUN

TV _____ in _____-definition on an
PLURAL NOUN   ADJECTIVE

LCD _____.
NOUN

1. If you have _____ friends who are in short supply
ADJECTIVE

of self-esteem, buy them a talking _____. With the
NOUN

push of a/an _____, it will say things like, "You're so
NOUN

_____!" and "You're the best _____ ever!"
ADJECTIVE   NOUN

From WE WISH YOU A MERRY MAD LIBS® • Copyright © 2010 by Penguin Random House LLC.

MAD LIBS® is fun to play with friends, but you can also play it by yourself! To begin with, DO NOT look at the story on the page below. Fill in the blanks on this page with the words called for. Then, using the words you have selected, fill in the blank spaces in the story.

Now you've created your own hilarious MAD LIBS® game!

TAKING CARE OF YOUR REINDEER

ADJECTIVE _____

ADJECTIVE _____

NOUN _____

ADJECTIVE _____

NUMBER _____

ADJECTIVE _____

PLURAL NOUN _____

ADJECTIVE _____

NOUN _____

ADJECTIVE _____

NUMBER _____

ADVERB _____

ADJECTIVE _____

NOUN _____

NOUN _____

ADVERB _____

ADJECTIVE _____

Congratulations! We hear you've adopted a/an ＿＿＿＿＿＿ reindeer.
<u>ADJECTIVE</u>

They make ＿＿＿＿＿＿ pets—but they require a lot of care and
<u>ADJECTIVE</u>

＿＿＿＿＿＿. Here are some tips for keeping your reindeer happy
<u>NOUN</u>

and ＿＿＿＿＿＿:
<u>ADJECTIVE</u>

• Feed it ＿＿＿＿＿＿ times a day. Not difficult to do, as
  <u>NUMBER</u>

  reindeer have a very ＿＿＿＿＿＿ diet. They eat grasses,
  <u>ADJECTIVE</u>

  moss, and ＿＿＿＿＿＿.
  <u>PLURAL NOUN</u>

• Make sure your reindeer gets ＿＿＿＿＿＿ exercise. In the
  <u>ADJECTIVE</u>

  wild, they travel farther than any other land ＿＿＿＿＿＿.
  <u>NOUN</u>

  They go on ＿＿＿＿＿＿ migrations, sometimes covering
  <u>ADJECTIVE</u>

  ＿＿＿＿＿＿ miles.
  <u>NUMBER</u>

• Groom your reindeer ＿＿＿＿＿＿. Its ＿＿＿＿＿＿
  <u>ADVERB</u>   <u>ADJECTIVE</u>

  antlers are covered in delicate ＿＿＿＿＿＿, which you can
  <u>NOUN</u>

  clean with a soft ＿＿＿＿＿＿. You should also brush its coat
  <u>NOUN</u>

  ＿＿＿＿＿＿ once a month.
  <u>ADVERB</u>

• Take your reindeer to the vet often to make sure it stays healthy

  and ＿＿＿＿＿＿.
  <u>ADJECTIVE</u>

MAD LIBS® is fun to play with friends, but you can also play it by yourself! To begin with, DO NOT look at the story on the page below. Fill in the blanks on this page with the words called for. Then, using the words you have selected, fill in the blank spaces in the story.

Now you've created your own hilarious MAD LIBS® game!

GET TO KNOW MRS. CLAUS

ADJECTIVE _____

NOUN _____

FIRST NAME (FEMALE) _____

NOUN _____

LAST NAME _____

ADJECTIVE _____

PLURAL NOUN _____

PLURAL NOUN _____

NOUN _____

NOUN _____

NOUN _____

NOUN _____

PART OF THE BODY (PLURAL) _____

ADJECTIVE _____

ADJECTIVE _____

ADJECTIVE _____

MAD LIBS®

GET TO KNOW MRS. CLAUS

Here are some _____ facts you may not know about me,
<u>ADJECTIVE</u>

Santa Claus's dear _____:
<u>NOUN</u>

Full name: Mrs. _____ Claus
<u>FIRST NAME (FEMALE)</u>

Hometown: The North _____
<u>NOUN</u>

Activities: Helping my husband, Santa _____, get ready for
<u>LAST NAME</u>

Christmas and taking care of the _____ elves
<u>ADJECTIVE</u>

Interests: Baking Christmas _____ and knitting _____
<u>PLURAL NOUN</u>   <u>PLURAL NOUN</u>

Favorite movies: *It's a Wonderful* _____, *Rudolph the Red-Nosed*
<u>NOUN</u>

_____
<u>NOUN</u>

Favorite books: *The* _____ *Before Christmas, How the*
<u>NOUN</u>

_____ *Stole Christmas*
<u>NOUN</u>

Favorite quotation: "All I want for Christmas is my two front

_____."
<u>PART OF THE BODY (PLURAL)</u>

About me: Have you ever wondered who brings _____ Santa
<u>ADJECTIVE</u>

his _____ gifts on Christmas Eve? Well, surprise! It's little
<u>ADJECTIVE</u>

_____ me!
<u>ADJECTIVE</u>

MAD LIBS® is fun to play with friends, but you can also play it by yourself! To begin with, DO NOT look at the story on the page below. Fill in the blanks on this page with the words called for. Then, using the words you have selected, fill in the blank spaces in the story.

Now you've created your own hilarious MAD LIBS® game!

CHRISTMAS FUNNIES

ADJECTIVE _____

ADJECTIVE _____

ADJECTIVE _____

NOUN _____

NOUN _____

ADJECTIVE _____

NOUN _____

PLURAL NOUN _____

ADJECTIVE _____

FIRST NAME _____

MAD LIBS®

CHRISTMAS FUNNIES

Q: What do you get when you cross a/an _____ vampire with
ADJECTIVE

a/an _____ snowman?
ADJECTIVE

A: Frostbite!

Q: Why did the _____ reindeer cross the _____?
ADJECTIVE   NOUN

A: To get to the other _____!
NOUN

Q: What do _____ elves sing to Santa?
ADJECTIVE

A: "*Freeze* a Jolly Good _____."
NOUN

Q: What do polar _____ eat for lunch?
PLURAL NOUN

A: *Iceberg*-ers!

Q: What do you call a/an _____ person who is afraid of
ADJECTIVE

_____ Claus?
FIRST NAME

A: *Claus*trophobic.

MAD LIBS® is fun to play with friends, but you can also play it by yourself! To begin with, DO NOT look at the story on the page below. Fill in the blanks on this page with the words called for. Then, using the words you have selected, fill in the blank spaces in the story.

Now you've created your own hilarious MAD LIBS® game!

CHRISTMAS AROUND THE WORLD, PART 1

ADJECTIVE _____

PLURAL NOUN _____

NOUN _____

ADJECTIVE _____

PLURAL NOUN _____

ADVERB _____

NOUN _____

NOUN _____

NOUN _____

PLURAL NOUN _____

PLURAL NOUN _____

ADJECTIVE _____

ADJECTIVE _____

ADJECTIVE _____

PLURAL NOUN _____

PLURAL NOUN _____

PLURAL NOUN _____

MAD LIBS

CHRISTMAS AROUND THE WORLD, PART 1

Americans have many _____ Christmas traditions. They
ADJECTIVE

decorate Christmas _____, sing _____ carols,
PLURAL NOUN   NOUN

and have _____ Christmas dinners with their families. But
ADJECTIVE

how do _____ around the world celebrate?
PLURAL NOUN

- In **Sweden**, they _____ celebrate St. Lucia's Day before
ADVERB

Christmas. The youngest _____ in the family wears
NOUN

a white _____, a red _____, and a crown of
NOUN   NOUN

_____ with candles in it. She then serves coffee
PLURAL NOUN

and _____ to everyone in her _____
PLURAL NOUN   ADJECTIVE

family.

- In **Australia**, it is hot and _____ at Christmastime,
ADJECTIVE

because this _____ holiday falls in the middle of their
ADJECTIVE

summer. _____ gather outside at night to light
PLURAL NOUN

_____ and sing Christmas _____.
PLURAL NOUN   PLURAL NOUN

MAD LIBS® is fun to play with friends, but you can also play it by yourself! To begin with, DO NOT look at the story on the page below. Fill in the blanks on this page with the words called for. Then, using the words you have selected, fill in the blank spaces in the story.

Now you've created your own hilarious MAD LIBS® game!

CHRISTMAS AROUND THE WORLD, PART 2

ADJECTIVE _____

PLURAL NOUN _____

ADJECTIVE _____

ADJECTIVE _____

PLURAL NOUN _____

PLURAL NOUN _____

ADJECTIVE _____

PLURAL NOUN _____

ADJECTIVE _____

NOUN _____

PLURAL NOUN _____

NOUN _____

NOUN _____

NOUN _____

PLURAL NOUN _____

MAD☺LIBS
CHRISTMAS AROUND
THE WORLD, PART 2

- In **China**, people decorate their _____ homes with
  ADJECTIVE

  paper _____. They also put up _____ trees
  PLURAL NOUN   ADJECTIVE

  decorated with _____ lanterns, _____,
  ADJECTIVE   PLURAL NOUN

  and red _____.
  PLURAL NOUN

- In **Mexico**, children look forward to a/an _____
  ADJECTIVE

  party where young _____ take turns hitting a/an
  PLURAL NOUN

  _____ piñata with a/an _____, until all the
  ADJECTIVE   NOUN

  _____ and other treats fall out.
  PLURAL NOUN

- In **Germany**, families celebrate the weeks leading up to

  Christmas with an Advent _____. Each Sunday, they
  NOUN

  light another _____ in the wreath. Before Christmas,
  NOUN

  Germans celebrate St. Nicholas Day, where kids put a/an

  _____ outside their door at night, and in the morning
  NOUN

  it is filled with candy and _____.
  PLURAL NOUN

MAD LIBS® is fun to play with friends, but you can also play it by yourself! To begin with, DO NOT look at the story on the page below. Fill in the blanks on this page with the words called for. Then, using the words you have selected, fill in the blank spaces in the story.

Now you've created your own hilarious MAD LIBS® game!

A TROPICAL CHRISTMAS

PLURAL NOUN _____

NOUN _____

A PLACE _____

PLURAL NOUN _____

ADJECTIVE _____

NOUN _____

NOUN _____

PLURAL NOUN _____

ADJECTIVE _____

ADJECTIVE _____

PLURAL NOUN _____

ADJECTIVE _____

NOUN _____

ADJECTIVE _____

NOUN _____

NOUN _____

ADJECTIVE _____

MAD LIBS®

A TROPICAL CHRISTMAS

Some _____ can't imagine celebrating Christmas where

PLURAL NOUN

there's no snow falling from the _____. But it's not all bad!

NOUN

Here in (the) _____, where it's always sunny, we decorate

A PLACE

palm _____ with _____ lights instead of decorating a

PLURAL NOUN   ADJECTIVE

pine _____. Instead of making a snow-_____, we

NOUN   NOUN

make _____ out of sand. Best of all, we don't have to

PLURAL NOUN

bundle up against the _____ wind and the _____

ADJECTIVE   ADJECTIVE

cold and freeze our _____ off. At Christmas, we happily

PLURAL NOUN

splash around in the _____ ocean and bask in the

ADJECTIVE

_____-shine. Or we go surfing and catch _____

NOUN   ADJECTIVE

waves. As you can see, I no longer dream of a white _____.

NOUN

I'm happy celebrating Christmas on a sandy _____ in the

NOUN

_____ sun!

ADJECTIVE

MAD LIBS® is fun to play with friends, but you can also play it by yourself! To begin with, DO NOT look at the story on the page below. Fill in the blanks on this page with the words called for. Then, using the words you have selected, fill in the blank spaces in the story.

Now you've created your own hilarious MAD LIBS® game!

CHRISTMAS IN JULY

LAST NAME _____

ADJECTIVE _____

A PLACE _____

NOUN _____

PLURAL NOUN _____

ADVERB _____

NUMBER _____

ADJECTIVE _____

NOUN _____

NOUN _____

PLURAL NOUN _____

ADJECTIVE _____

VERB _____

NOUN _____

MAD LIBS®

CHRISTMAS IN JULY

Hurry on down to _____ Furniture for our _____
LAST NAME   ADJECTIVE

Christmas-in-July sale! Yes, folks, Christmas has come early here in

(the) _____, and we're celebrating with _____-wide
A PLACE   NOUN

savings on couches, tables, and _____! With prices
PLURAL NOUN

_____ reduced up to _____ percent off, you can't
ADVERB   NUMBER

afford to miss this _____ event! Purchase any _____
ADJECTIVE   NOUN

in the store with no down _____ and no _____
NOUN   PLURAL NOUN

for twelve months. But our _____ sale only lasts through
ADJECTIVE

Thursday. So don't delay! _____ on down today, and have a
VERB

merry _____ in July!
NOUN

MAD LIBS® is fun to play with friends, but you can also play it by yourself! To begin with, DO NOT look at the story on the page below. Fill in the blanks on this page with the words called for. Then, using the words you have selected, fill in the blank spaces in the story.

Now you've created your own hilarious MAD LIBS® game!

ELVES WANTED

PLURAL NOUN _____

NUMBER _____

ADJECTIVE _____

VERB _____

NOUN _____

PLURAL NOUN _____

NOUN _____

ADJECTIVE _____

NOUN _____

ADJECTIVE _____

ADJECTIVE _____

VERB _____

PLURAL NOUN _____

A PLACE _____

PART OF THE BODY (PLURAL) _____

MAD LIBS

ELVES WANTED

Attention, all _____ ! Santa Claus is looking for _____
PLURAL NOUN   NUMBER

_____ elves to _____ in his workshop at the North
ADJECTIVE   VERB

_____ . Job responsibilities include making toy
NOUN

_____ faster than the speed of _____; taking care
PLURAL NOUN   NOUN

of eight _____ reindeer when it is necessary; repairing Santa's
ADJECTIVE

shiny red _____; and, of course, sorting letters from
NOUN

_____ girls and boys. Some very _____ elves might
ADJECTIVE   ADJECTIVE

get the chance to _____ in Santa's sleigh on Christmas Eve
VERB

and help him deliver _____ all over (the) _____.
PLURAL NOUN   A PLACE

Most importantly, candidates' _____ must be full of
PART OF THE BODY (PLURAL)

Christmas cheer!

MAD LIBS® is fun to play with friends, but you can also play it by yourself! To begin with, DO NOT look at the story on the page below. Fill in the blanks on this page with the words called for. Then, using the words you have selected, fill in the blank spaces in the story.

Now you've created your own hilarious MAD LIBS® game!

SNOW DAY!

NOUN _____

ADJECTIVE _____

NOUN _____

ADJECTIVE _____

NOUN _____

ADJECTIVE _____

NOUN _____

NOUN _____

NOUN _____

NOUN _____

NOUN _____

VERB _____

ADJECTIVE _____

PLURAL NOUN _____

NOUN _____

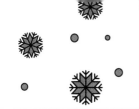

MAD LIBS

SNOW DAY!

This is your lucky _____. Because of the _____
              NOUN   ADJECTIVE

blizzard, school's been canceled. So how will you spend this unexpected

_____? Here are some _____ suggestions:
   NOUN   ADJECTIVE

- Stay inside and drink hot _____ while watching
                               NOUN

  _____ cartoons on television.
  ADJECTIVE

- Grab your _____ and go sledding down a steep
              NOUN

  _____.
  NOUN

- Find a frozen _____ and go ice-skating on it.
          NOUN

- Build a/an _____ fort. Construct walls out of hard-
          NOUN

  packed _____, then _____ inside for
      NOUN   VERB

  hours on end.

- Break up into _____ teams and have a snowball fight
         ADJECTIVE

  with your neighborhood _____.
                 PLURAL NOUN

- Sleep the _____ away.
      NOUN

MAD LIBS® is fun to play with friends, but you can also play it by yourself! To begin with, DO NOT look at the story on the page below. Fill in the blanks on this page with the words called for. Then, using the words you have selected, fill in the blank spaces in the story.

Now you've created your own hilarious MAD LIBS® game!

THE NUTCRACKER

ADJECTIVE _____

NOUN _____

NOUN _____

ADJECTIVE _____

ADJECTIVE _____

NOUN _____

ADJECTIVE _____

PLURAL NOUN _____

ADJECTIVE _____

PLURAL NOUN _____

TYPE OF FOOD _____

TYPE OF LIQUID _____

VERB ENDING IN "ING" _____

ADJECTIVE _____

ADJECTIVE _____

THE NUTCRACKER

The Nutcracker is a famous ballet that tells the _____ story of
ADJECTIVE

a little _____ named Clara whose godfather gives her a/an
NOUN

_____-cracker for Christmas. Amazingly, the nutcracker
NOUN

comes to life as a/an _____ prince who rescues Clara from
ADJECTIVE

some very _____ mice. Then Clara and her prince travel to a
ADJECTIVE

magical _____, where they are greeted by _____
NOUN   ADJECTIVE

snowflakes and dancing _____. They continue their enchanted
PLURAL NOUN

journey and enter the _____ land of the Sugar Plum
ADJECTIVE

_____, where people dressed like _____ and
PLURAL NOUN   TYPE OF FOOD

_____ dance for them. When the festivities are over, Clara
TYPE OF LIQUID

finds herself at home, _____ under the Christmas tree
VERB ENDING IN "ING"

and holding her _____ nutcracker. It was all just a/an
ADJECTIVE

_____ dream!
ADJECTIVE

MAD LIBS® is fun to play with friends, but you can also play it by yourself! To begin with, DO NOT look at the story on the page below. Fill in the blanks on this page with the words called for. Then, using the words you have selected, fill in the blank spaces in the story.

Now you've created your own hilarious MAD LIBS® game!

SANTA TALKS

NOUN _____

ADJECTIVE _____

NOUN _____

NOUN _____

NOUN _____

PLURAL NOUN _____

NUMBER _____

PLURAL NOUN _____

PART OF THE BODY _____

NOUN _____

ADJECTIVE _____

PLURAL NOUN _____

ADJECTIVE _____

ADJECTIVE _____

ADJECTIVE _____

MAD LIBS

SANTA TALKS

The following is an exclusive interview at the North _____
                                                         NOUN

with the rotund man in the _____ suit:
                              ADJECTIVE

Q: You are described as a jolly _____. Are you that way 24/7?
                                      NOUN

Santa: Ho, ho, ho. Does that answer your _____?
                                                NOUN

Q: My next _____ may be somewhat embarrassing. Have you
                  NOUN

put on some extra _____ recently?
                     PLURAL NOUN

Santa: I'm actually at my average weight of _____ pounds.
                                                   NUMBER

Q: Doesn't that make it difficult for you to get down chimneys,

especially carrying a sack full of children's _____?
                                                 PLURAL NOUN

Santa: No, I just suck in my _____ and squeeze down the
                                   PART OF THE BODY

_____. I'm sorry, we're going to have to cut this _____
     NOUN   ADJECTIVE

interview short. I've got to get all the kids' _____ delivered.
                                                  PLURAL NOUN

Q: Wait—how do you get around the _____ world in one night?
                                         ADJECTIVE

Santa: I have a/an _____ sleigh and a/an _____ team
                         ADJECTIVE   ADJECTIVE

of reindeer—and remember, most of the world is downhill these days.

Ho, ho, ho!

From WE WISH YOU A MERRY MAD LIBS® • Copyright © 2010 by Penguin Random House LLC.

MAD LIBS® is fun to play with friends, but you can also play it by yourself! To begin with, DO NOT look at the story on the page below. Fill in the blanks on this page with the words called for. Then, using the words you have selected, fill in the blank spaces in the story.

Now you've created your own hilarious MAD LIBS® game!

CHRISTMAS COOKIES

NOUN _____

NOUN _____

PLURAL NOUN _____

PLURAL NOUN _____

PLURAL NOUN _____

PLURAL NOUN _____

PLURAL NOUN _____

PLURAL NOUN _____

NOUN _____

PLURAL NOUN _____

NOUN _____

ADJECTIVE _____

ADJECTIVE _____

ADVERB _____

ADJECTIVE _____

ADJECTIVE _____

ADJECTIVE _____

MAD LIBS

CHRISTMAS COOKIES

Whether red or green, covered with sprinkles or just plain old

_____, Christmas cookies are the _____'s meow!

NOUN   NOUN

Some of the tastiest of these _____ include:

PLURAL NOUN

• Sugar _____: These rank as one of the most

PLURAL NOUN

  popular Christmas _____. They are often shaped

PLURAL NOUN

  like Christmas _____ and _____, with

PLURAL NOUN   PLURAL NOUN

  frosting and _____ sprinkled on top.

PLURAL NOUN

• _____ macaroons: These coconut _____

NOUN   PLURAL NOUN

  delight the _____-buds, especially when they've been

NOUN

  dipped in rich and _____ chocolate.

ADJECTIVE

• Gingerbread cookies: Who can resist the _____ aroma of

ADJECTIVE

  these _____ baked spicy classics? At Christmastime

ADVERB

  they are usually cut into the shape of _____ girls

ADJECTIVE

  and _____ boys, and many families also build

ADJECTIVE

  _____ gingerbread houses.

ADJECTIVE

MAD LIBS® is fun to play with friends, but you can also play it by yourself! To begin with, DO NOT look at the story on the page below. Fill in the blanks on this page with the words called for. Then, using the words you have selected, fill in the blank spaces in the story.

Now you've created your own hilarious MAD LIBS® game!

HOLIDAY ADVICE COLUMN

PERSON IN ROOM (FEMALE) _____

ADVERB _____

PERSON IN ROOM _____

NOUN _____

NOUN _____

ADJECTIVE _____

NOUN _____

NOUN _____

ADVERB _____

ADJECTIVE _____

A PLACE _____

SAME ADJECTIVE _____

ADJECTIVE _____

A PLACE _____

PART OF THE BODY _____

NOUN _____

A PLACE _____

ADJECTIVE _____

MAD LIBS®

HOLIDAY ADVICE COLUMN

Dear Miss _____,
PERSON IN ROOM (FEMALE)

I _____ need your advice. I have to buy a Christmas present
ADVERB

for my friend _____. We've known each other since the first
PERSON IN ROOM

day of _____ school, and he/she means the _____ to
NOUN _NOUN_

me. So here's my _____ problem—my friend already owns
ADJECTIVE

every _____ known to man. What do I get for the
NOUN

_____ who has everything? _____ yours,
NOUN _ADVERB_

_____ in (the) _____.
ADJECTIVE _A PLACE_

Dear _____,
SAME ADJECTIVE

The solution to your _____ dilemma is easy! We're talking
ADJECTIVE

about your best friend in all of (the) _____. It doesn't matter
A PLACE

what you give—so long as it comes from the _____. Try
PART OF THE BODY

making your friend a homemade _____, or give him/her a
NOUN

gift certificate to (the) _____. No matter what you decide,
A PLACE

your friend will appreciate the _____ thought.
ADJECTIVE

MAD LIBS® is fun to play with friends, but you can also play it by yourself! To begin with, DO NOT look at the story on the page below. Fill in the blanks on this page with the words called for. Then, using the words you have selected, fill in the blank spaces in the story.

Now you've created your own hilarious MAD LIBS® game!

A SPECIAL RECIPE FOR HOT CHOCOLATE

ADJECTIVE _____

PART OF THE BODY (PLURAL) _____

PLURAL NOUN _____

ADJECTIVE _____

TYPE OF LIQUID _____

NOUN _____

NOUN _____

ADJECTIVE _____

NUMBER _____

NUMBER _____

ADVERB _____

ADJECTIVE _____

NOUN _____

NOUN _____

ADJECTIVE _____

NOUN _____

MAD☺LIBS®
A SPECIAL RECIPE FOR
HOT CHOCOLATE

There is nothing more comforting than a/an _____, frothy
                                          ADJECTIVE

hot chocolate to warm up your _____on the coldest
                              PART OF THE BODY (PLURAL)

_____ of winter. Here is a recipe that has been passed down
PLURAL NOUN

from generation to generation in my _____ family. Pour one
                                    ADJECTIVE

cup of _____, one _____ of half-and-half, one
       TYPE OF LIQUID   NOUN

tablespoon of vanilla, and two ounces of semisweet _____
                                                   NOUN

into a/an _____ pan. Place it on the stove and heat at
          ADJECTIVE

_____ degrees for _____ minutes. Stir _____
NUMBER   NUMBER   ADVERB

until the chocolate melts. Pour the liquid into two _____
                                                    ADJECTIVE

mugs and serve with a dollop of whipped _____ on top. If
                                        NOUN

you add some atmosphere, your _____ will taste even better:
                              NOUN

Enjoy your drink in front of a/an _____ fireplace or while
                                  ADJECTIVE

watching the _____-flakes fall outside your window.
             NOUN

From WE WISH YOU A MERRY MAD LIBS® • Copyright © 2010 by Penguin Random House LLC.

MAD LIBS® is fun to play with friends, but you can also play it by yourself! To begin with, DO NOT look at the story on the page below. Fill in the blanks on this page with the words called for. Then, using the words you have selected, fill in the blank spaces in the story.

Now you've created your own hilarious MAD LIBS® game!

HOW TO MAKE A SNOWMAN

ADJECTIVE _____

PLURAL NOUN _____

ADJECTIVE _____

ADJECTIVE _____

PART OF THE BODY _____

NOUN _____

ADJECTIVE _____

PLURAL NOUN _____

PART OF THE BODY (PLURAL) _____

NOUN _____

PART OF THE BODY _____

NOUN _____

NOUN _____

PLURAL NOUN _____

NOUN _____

ADJECTIVE _____

NOUN _____

MAD LIBS®
HOW TO MAKE
A SNOWMAN

Want to make a/an _____ snowman? All you need is some
                      ADJECTIVE

snow and a few household _____. Then just follow this
                            PLURAL NOUN

_____ step-by-step guide:
ADJECTIVE

- Roll three _____ balls out of snow: one for the base, one
              ADJECTIVE

  for the torso, and one for the _____. Then pile them
                                  PART OF THE BODY

  on top of one another so they resemble a/an _____.
                                                NOUN

- To complete your snowman's _____ body, use some
                               ADJECTIVE

  long, thin _____ for arms and give him a pair of
              PLURAL NOUN

  _____ made of coal. Then add a button
  PART OF THE BODY (PLURAL)

  _____ and a carrot _____.
  NOUN   PART OF THE BODY

- You can accessorize your snowy creation with a corncob

  _____, a stovepipe _____, and some buttons
  NOUN   NOUN

  made of _____. If it's really cold outside, you can
           PLURAL NOUN

  give him a knitted _____.
                      NOUN

- And don't forget to give your snowman a name! _____
                                                  ADJECTIVE

  the _____-man is always a popular choice.
       NOUN

MAD LIBS® is fun to play with friends, but you can also play it by yourself! To begin with, DO NOT look at the story on the page below. Fill in the blanks on this page with the words called for. Then, using the words you have selected, fill in the blank spaces in the story.

Now you've created your own hilarious MAD LIBS® game!

ELF-MAIL

PERSON IN ROOM _____

PERSON IN ROOM _____

ADJECTIVE _____

ADJECTIVE _____

ADJECTIVE _____

PLURAL NOUN _____

ADJECTIVE _____

PERSON IN ROOM _____

NOUN _____

ADJECTIVE _____

ADJECTIVE _____

PERSON IN ROOM _____

NOUN _____

VERB _____

PLURAL NOUN _____

MAD LIBS®

ELF-MAIL

To: _____-elf@santasworkshop.elf
       PERSON IN ROOM

From: _____ slittlehelper@santasworkshop.elf
         PERSON IN ROOM

Hi there, _____ buddy! Just wanted to drop you a/an
                ADJECTIVE

_____ note to see how you are doing. It's been a/an
 ADJECTIVE

_____ Christmas season here. I've made so many toys—
 ADJECTIVE

especially jack-in-the-_____—that I've lost count! On
                          PLURAL NOUN

another _____ note, are you getting excited about
          ADJECTIVE

_____'s Christmas Eve elf party? I hear DJ _____ Elf
 PERSON IN ROOM   NOUN

will be spinning some really _____ Christmas tunes! I've also
                               ADJECTIVE

got some _____ gossip: I hear _____ is a shoo-in for
          ADJECTIVE   PERSON IN ROOM

Elf of the Year! He/She totally deserves it for being such a hardworking

_____. Well, I've gotta _____—it's back to the
 NOUN   VERB

_____ at the workshop. See you soon!
 PLURAL NOUN

MAD LIBS® is fun to play with friends, but you can also play it by yourself! To begin with, DO NOT look at the story on the page below. Fill in the blanks on this page with the words called for. Then, using the words you have selected, fill in the blank spaces in the story.

Now you've created your own hilarious MAD LIBS® game!

A CHRISTMAS CARD

ADJECTIVE _____

ADJECTIVE _____

NOUN _____

NOUN _____

ADJECTIVE _____

PLURAL NOUN _____

PLURAL NOUN _____

ADJECTIVE _____

NOUN _____

ADJECTIVE _____

VERB _____

ADJECTIVE _____

NOUN _____

PLURAL NOUN _____

NOUN _____

NOUN _____

PERSON IN ROOM _____

MAD LIBS

A CHRISTMAS CARD

Dear Grandma and Grandpa,

Merry Christmas to my wonderful, _____ grandparents. Our
                                    ADJECTIVE

house is filled with _____ Christmas spirit. Yesterday, we went
                          ADJECTIVE

to the _____ farm and bought a ten-foot-tall _____.
          NOUN   NOUN

We put it in our _____ living room and covered it with lights
                      ADJECTIVE

and _____. Dad decorated the front of the house with
         PLURAL NOUN

strings of _____ and _____ decorations. And
               PLURAL NOUN   ADJECTIVE

Mom baked a lot of _____ cookies that smell absolutely
                          NOUN

_____! I hope you're excited about coming to _____
   ADJECTIVE   VERB

with us! I can't wait to see you at our _____ Christmas dinner.
                                              ADJECTIVE

We're having your favorite—roast _____ and mashed
                                        NOUN

_____! And, of course, _____ pie for dessert!
   PLURAL NOUN   NOUN

Love from your grand- _____,
                            NOUN

_____
PERSON IN ROOM

Join the millions of Mad Libs fans creating
wacky and wonderful stories on our apps!

Download Mad Libs today!